To my Friends Don & Margot

Be blessed as you... a blessing to me.

William G. Pooh

In Spirit And In Truth

William G. Poole

EDITED BY
PAMELA PEDERSEN

WESTBOW
PRESS
A DIVISION OF THOMAS NELSON

WestBow Press books may be ordered through booksellers or by contacting:

WestBow Press
A Division of Thomas Nelson
1663 Liberty Drive
Bloomington, IN 47403
www.westbowpress.com
1-(866) 928-1240

ISBN: 978-1-4497-3583-8 (sc)
ISBN: 978-1-4497-3584-5 (hc)
ISBN: 978-1-4497-3585-2 (e)

Library of Congress Control Number: 2011963332

Printed in the United States of America

WestBow Press rev. date: 01/27/2012

Introduction

As I sit and think about this book I have to take account as to just how much I need to change still in my life. The words of John the Baptist "I must decrease He must increase" ring true to my heart. There are those who have gone before us that were acutely aware of God's presence around them 24/7, and I know that this is God's desire for each of His children today.

I have seen where the Spirit of God has moved in such a mighty way that everyone in the service was touched and moved by Him. I have seen where everyone in the service was also touched and moved in a similar way by man. What is the difference?

I have been in secular concerts where the atmosphere was so spiritually charged that you would think that you were at a Pentecostal-type Church. I have met secular people who are more aware of the spiritual world around them than a lot of people who profess to be Christians are. Christians, who love Jesus very much, but seem to not have the slightest idea that another realm outside their physical realm exists.

What is the difference? What makes us aware of God in our minds and hearts, but unaware of His presence in our everyday life? The original man Adam was created to be in God's presence without hindrance. He enjoyed the fullness of God's presence 24/7 until the Fall came when the veil of sin came between them. When Jesus died on the cross, His sacrifice caused the veil that separated man from God to be torn in two. We now have the means by which we can come before our God and into His presence any time we wish. So what is stopping us?

In this book we will look at how to experience and live in the reality of God's presence, as well as how this can change our lives and those around us. We will also look at how God has laid out a "blueprint" of how we are to come into His presence, what He wants to do when we are there, and the importance of music and the role it plays in a lifestyle of worship.

Acknowledgments

I would first and foremost like to thank my best friend, Jesus who sought me out, encouraged me when I wanted to quit, and put up with all my "buts". I would also like to thank Jolande, my wife, who believed in me when no one else would, and endured me hiding in my office in order to write this. To all those who had came before me with this message, I am indebted to your work, and I hope I have done it justice. I would also like to thank my friend Ray for teaching me humility in worship, and Dr. Charlotte Baker for her obedience to the Father, which made her a mentor in my life long before we ever met. I also would like to thank my editor, Pam, who painstakingly corrected all my mistakes, as well as Lorna, my cover designer who risked and told me the truth, so not to let me go on and make a great mistake.

Last but not least I would like to dedicate this work to my late stepdaughter Joanna, whose endurance through suffering inspires me even to this day.

Garcon

Contents

CHAPTER ONE

Going Past The Veil

"With a loud cry, Jesus breathed his last. The curtain of the temple was torn in two from top to bottom. And when the centurion, who stood there in front of Jesus, heard his cry and saw how he died, he said, "Surely this man was the Son of God!" (Mark 15:37-39)

"Now the LORD God had planted a garden in the east, in Eden; and there he put the man he had formed. And the LORD God made all kinds of trees grow out of the ground—trees that were pleasing to the eye and *good for food. In the middle of the garden were the tree of life and the tree of the knowledge of good and evil."* (Gen. 2:8-9)

In Genesis 2:8-9, the Bible talks about a special place that God had designed where He would commune with man, a garden, with trees that were pleasing to the eye and good for food. This points out the fact that all the plants in the garden could be seen and felt, and were as real to Adam as any plant we have today. It also says that the tree of life and the tree of good and evil were there in the middle of the garden. According to Genesis 3:22 when you ate of the tree of good and evil, your mind was able conceive the difference between good and evil. Also when you ate of the tree of life you would receive eternal life. This constitutes a spiritual condition that happens in a physical realm.

In Genesis 3:8 it says that Adam and Eve <u>heard</u> God walking in the garden. How can this be unless Adam had the ability to see, hear, and touch the spiritual aspects of God?

Charles Spurgeon when describing the Garden of Eden put it this way,

> "What a glorious state this world was in at the very first, *in the age of Paradise,* for the Lord was there! Our glorious Creator, having taken

the first days of the week to make the world, and fit it up for man, did not bring forward his dear child until the house was built and furnished, and supplied for his use and happiness. He did not put him in the garden to dress it till the roses were blooming, and the fruits were ripe. When the table was furnished he introduced the guest, by saying, "Let us make man in our image, after our likeness." The Lord put man, not in an unreclaimed plot of soil, where he must hunger till he could produce a harvest; but into an Eden of delights, where he was at home, with creatures of every sort to attend him. He had not to water dry lands, nor need he thirst himself, for four rivers flowed through his royal domain, rippling over sands of gold. I might say much of that fair garden of innocence and bliss, but the best thing I could say would be the Lord was there. "The Lord God walked in the garden in the cool of the day," and communed with man; and man, being innocent, held high converse with his condescending Maker. The topstone of the bliss of Paradise was

this all-comprehending privilege—
the Lord is there." (C. H. Spurgeon
1891)

Some would say that Eden was not a real
place and that it was just a nice story. If that
were true then why would the Bible give a fairly
good description of where Eden was?

> "A river watering the garden flowed
> from Eden; from there it was
> separated into four headwaters. The
> name of the first is the Pishon; it
> winds through the entire land of
> Havilah, where there is gold. (The
> gold of that land is good; aromatic
> resin and onyx are also there.) The
> name of the second river is the Gihon;
> it winds through the entire land of
> Cush. The name of the third river is
> the Tigris; it runs along the east side
> of Asshur. And the fourth river is the
> Euphrates." (Gen. 2:10-14)

All this points to an area called the Armenian
Highland bordering on the northeast part of
Turkey and Armenia. If this is true then why
have we not found this garden yet? Some would
say that the flood destroyed Eden, and yet Jesus
states in Rev 2:7 "I will give the right to eat

from the tree of life, which is in the paradise of God."

The answer can only be that it is a garden that is physical but also spiritual, in that it cannot be seen by our physical eye. Adam was a man who could see and touch both the physical realm and the spiritual realm of this world, and of God's. Due to the fall of man sin has placed a veil between God and Adam, to the point that after he left Eden he was no longer able to touch or see it. This veil grew to the point that man no longer was able to naturally see God, unless he revealed Himself to man in a physically manifested way.

> "There was no veil in Paradise between man and God. There were three places or regions; the outer earth, Eden, and "the Garden of Eden", or Paradise; but there was no veil nor fence between, hindering access from the one to the other. There was nothing to prevent man from going in to speak with God, or God from coming out to speak with man. It was not till after man had disobeyed that the veil was let down which separated God from man, which made a distinction

between the dwellings of man and the habitation of God.

Before God had spoken or done aught in the way of separation, man betrayed his consciousness of his new standing, and of the necessity for a covering or screen. He fled from God into the thick trees of the garden, that their foliage might hide him from God and God from him. In so doing he showed that he felt two things. 1. That there must be a veil between him and God; 2. That, now, in his altered position, distance from God (if such a thing could be) was his safety."

"Even if God had said "draw near," man could not have responded "let us draw near," or felt "it is good for me to draw near to God." For sin had now come between, and until that should be dealt with in the way of pardon and removal, he could not approach God, nor expect God to approach him." (Rent Veil / Bonar)

How this must have broken God's heart for man was made in His image, and was created to commune with Him. Now there was a veil hiding

His physical presence from man. But God had a plan! He would send His only begotten Son, to take the form of man, and tear that veil in two once and for all.

When John the Baptist came on the scene, for the first time in over four hundred years, a public prophetic voice was heard pronouncing that the Kingdom of Heaven was at hand. During Jesus' public life, the dead were being brought back to life, the sick were being healed, the blind were seeing and the deaf were hearing. In Luke 11:20 Jesus makes a significant statement and declares that the Kingdom of Heaven has come upon us. *"If I drive out demons by the finger of God, then the kingdom of God has come upon you."* What does this mean, and of what significance is it to us anyway?

Since the fall of man till this time and even now, men have realized that "we got to get ourselves back to the garden". (Woodstock, 1969, Cosby, Still, Nash and Young) The Garden being not so much a physical place as much as it was a place of communion with our Creator. The problem has been that we have been trying to get there on our own terms. In the Garden, Adam and Eve were at one with God and His world. They were in a physical relationship with God and could interact with the spiritual and physical world as if they were one and the same. Remember, they heard God walking in the garden. They could see and eat from the tree of good and evil, as well as the tree of life!

Through the occult and various other means including drugs, men have been interacting with the spiritual world, hoping to find this place of paradise, this place of connecting spiritually with God. Jesus was showing us that a spiritual reality was there, but Paradise could be only entered into on His terms.

When David wished to build God a house of cedar for God to dwell in, God saw in the future a temple that he would reside in, but not one built by man.

> "*The LORD declares to you that the LORD himself will establish a house for you. When your days are over and you rest with your fathers, I will raise up your offspring to succeed you, who will come from your own body, and I will establish his kingdom. He is the one who will build a house for my Name, and I will establish the throne of his kingdom forever.*" (2nd Samuel 7:11-13)

This whole prophecy has two fulfillments, and we can see them here in these verses. Both Solomon and Jesus were from the family of David, and both of their kingdoms were established: one physical, one spiritual.

Again both built a house for God to dwell in, one physical and one spiritual. Although both kingdoms were established, only the physical kingdom would not last forever, for we know that the Davidic line of kings to rule over the physical kingdom of Israel ceased with the fall of Jerusalem in 587 BC. But the spiritual kingdom of the line of David established through Jesus would last forever. *"With a loud cry, Jesus breathed his last. The curtain of the temple was torn in two from top to bottom!" (Mark 15:37-38)*

With the veil in Herod's temple in Jerusalem (a temple that symbolized the efforts of man to have a place to meet with God) torn in two from top to bottom there was nothing stopping a man from going into the Holy of Holies. If he did he would not find God's physical presence there, for God's manifested presence had left the temple long before. So if nothing was there why tear the veil in two? The answer is that God was showing mankind that He had provided a means to come back into His presence, to pass the veil that separated them from Him since the fall of mankind in the garden.

That provision came in the form of a wooden Roman cross, on which the Lamb of God performed the final sacrifice that would take away the sins of the world. (John 1:29)

"Consequently, just as the result of one trespass was condemnation for all men, so also the result of one act of righteousness was justification that brings life for all men. For just as through the disobedience of the one man the many were made sinners, so also through the obedience of the one man the many will be made righteous." (Romans 5:18-19)

Forty years before the final destruction of the physical temple, a new temple was being built. But unlike the physical temple it was a spiritual temple not made by mans hands, but by God Himself.

"As you come to him, the living Stone rejected by men but chosen by God and precious to him you also, like living stones, are being built into a spiritual house to be a holy priesthood, offering spiritual sacrifices acceptable to God through Jesus Christ. For in Scripture it says: 'See, I lay a stone in Zion, a chosen and precious cornerstone, and the one who trusts in him will never be put to shame.'" (1Peter 2:4-6)

How does one come to the place of entering into this temple, you might say? It is by accepting the sacrifice that Jesus made for us on the cross, and receiving Him into our hearts as our Savior, High Priest, and King. It is then that we are able to understand what Jesus meant in this verse.

> *"In reply Jesus declared, "I tell you the truth, no one can see the kingdom of God unless he is born again." "How can a man be born when he is old?" Nicodemus asked. "Surely he cannot enter a second time into his mother's womb to be born!" Jesus answered, "I tell you the truth, no one can enter the kingdom of God unless he is born of water and the Spirit. Flesh gives birth to flesh, but the Spirit gives birth to spirit. You should not be surprised at my saying, 'You must be born again.' The wind blows wherever it pleases. You hear its sound, but you cannot tell where it comes from or where it is going. So it is with everyone born of the Spirit."* (John 3:3-8)

God is beckoning His people to come to Him, enter in past the veil of sin and come into His presence, and walk with Him as we were created to do.

CHAPTER TWO

The Temple Old & New

When we look at the idea of a temple in any religion, it is generally considered a place where the resident god is worshiped. In most religions this god would be in the form of an idol, and it would be considered the place of dwelling for that god.

The Old Testament temple that we see in the Bible is also along the same lines of this, except for the fact that instead of an idol there was the Ark of the Covenant, and instead of a fallen angel posing as a deity, we have the true living Creator of the universe. The concept of God's presence inhabiting the temple was a forgone conclusion to the Jewish people during the period of the tabernacle and Solomon's temple, and was directly connected to the Ark of the Covenant.

When we look through the Old Testament, we see a description in regards to the different areas or courts in both the tabernacle, which was made by Moses, as well as Solomon's temple and Herod's temple. In each of these places of worship, we see that they had very similar structures. Each of them had four main areas, making up the temple grounds. The first area was a place for the general population to come; this area had no restrictions as to who could come and be there. This we will classify as the outer courts. Next was the area where people who were of Jewish decent could come and bring their sacrifices to the priest, who would offer them to God on their behalf. This area would be classified as the inner courts. The next area was called the Holy Place and it was where the priest would come and burn incense before God. In this area you would find the table of Presence, in which every seven days, or each Sabbath, the priest would bring in twelve loaves of "Shewbread" (Lev 24:5-6) and set them out on display upon the table, one loaf for each of the tribes of Israel. The last area was called the Holy of Holies and it was in this area that only the High Priest could come and offer a sacrifice before God on behalf of the nation of Israel. It was this area that the Presence of God was attributed to be inhabiting, and no one could go into the Holy of Holies except the High Priest, and he only once a year at that. Although the temple was a place where people would come to worship God, they were not able to enter into His presence.

To the Jews the temple was the center of their life; everything revolved around it. It was considered to be the most sacred piece of property in all the land, or for that fact, in the entire world. The location of the temple had great significance as well.

> "The present-day platform area of the Temple Mount lies topographically just below the peak of a Jerusalem ridge system known as Mount Moriah. This is the site David purchased from a Jebusite named Ornan late in his reign. King David prepared the area in order build a permanent House of God to replace the Tabernacle of Moses which accompanied the Jews after their Exodus from Egypt to the Promised Land." "The ridge system where the Temple Mount is now located is believed by many reputable sources to be the site where Abraham was told to sacrifice Isaac (Genesis

22:1-2). While Solomon built the First Temple about 3000 years ago, Abraham's visit to Mt. Moriah was about a thousand years earlier." (Dolphin & Kollen)

As we can see, the temple and the land it sat on has had a long history of significance to the Jewish people. It represented the physical identity of God's presence that was associated with the Temple, and the land it sat on made it the one place on earth where they could feel close to God.

Even with all it's beauty and grandeur it was only a shadow of what was to come (Hebrews 8:5) and with it's destruction 1939 years ago the man-made temple of God disappeared. Does this mean that there is no longer any place here on earth that God's presence resides in?

> *"The LORD declares to you that the LORD himself will establish a house for you. When your days are over and you rest with your fathers, I will raise up your offspring to succeed you, who will come from your own body, and I will establish his kingdom. He is the one who will build a house for my Name, and I will establish the throne of his kingdom forever. I will*

be his father, and he will be my son."
(2 Samuel 7:11-13)

If we were to just read this at face value, we would automatically come to the conclusion that the person whom God was referring to was King Solomon; after all, he did build the temple which God allowed His glory to fill 1 Kings 8:10-11. But if we dig a little further into this scripture we see something more. Verse 11 says that "the Lord himself will build a house" for David. This could be taken two ways; 1) a house being a metaphor referring to a family line, or 2) a house, a place of residence in which David (man) and God could abide together. I believe that this scripture was fulfilled in both senses, for it is common that prophetic scriptures can have more than one fulfillment. For example, the prophecy of the virgin being with child, that is found in Isaiah 7:13-17 we know had two fulfillments. The first fulfillment in Isaiah 8:3-4 and the second in the birth of Christ, the first being a shadow of the latter.

> *"Then Isaiah said, "Hear now, you house of David! Is it not enough to try the patience of humans? Will you try the patience of my God also? Therefore the Lord himself will give you a sign: The virgin will conceive and give birth to a son, and will call*

him Immanuel. He will be eating curds and honey when he knows enough to reject the wrong and choose the right, for before the boy knows enough to reject the wrong and choose the right, the land of the two kings you dread will be laid waste. The LORD will bring on you and on your people and on the house of your father a time unlike any since Ephraim broke away from Judah he will bring the king of Assyria." (Isaiah 7:13–17)

"Then I made love to the prophetess, and she conceived and gave birth to a son. And the LORD said to me, "Name him Maher-Shalal-Hash-Baz. For before the boy knows how to say 'My father' or 'My mother,' the wealth of Damascus and the plunder of Samaria will be carried off by the king of Assyria." (Isaiah 8:3-4)

Another example of this dual fulfillment is found in Daniel 9:27 where he speaks of the "abomination that causes desolation".

"He will confirm a covenant with many for one 'seven.' In the middle of the 'seven' he will put an end to

sacrifice and offering. And at the temple he will set up an abomination that causes desolation, until the end that is decreed is poured out on him." (Daniel 9:27)

When we look at the historical book of 1 Maccabees we see a fulfillment of this prophecy.

"And after that Antiochus had smitten Egypt, he returned again in the hundred forty and third year, and went up against Israel and Jerusalem with a great multitude, And entered proudly into the sanctuary, and took away the golden altar, and the candlestick of light, and all the vessels thereof, And the table of the shewbread, and the pouring vessels, and the vials. and the censers of gold, and the veil, and the crown, and the golden ornaments that were before the temple, all which he pulled off. He took also the silver and the gold, and the precious vessels: also he took the hidden treasures which he found. And when he had taken all away, he went into his own land, having made a great massacre, and spoken very proudly. Therefore there was a great mourning in Israel, in every place where they were;" "Now the fifteenth day of the month Casleu, in the hundred forty and fifth year, they set up the abomination of desolation upon the altar, and builded idol altars throughout the cities of Juda on every side;" "Now the five and twentieth day of the month they did sacrifice upon the idol altar, which was upon the altar of God." (1 Maccabees Chapter 1:20-25, 54, 59: KJV)

Yet when we read in Matthew 24 Jesus is describing the signs of the end of the times, and He refers to Daniel 9:27 in the future tense. This indicates, that according to Jesus, this prophecy is yet to be fulfilled in it entirety.

> *"So when you see standing in the holy place 'the abomination that causes desolation,' spoken of through the prophet Daniel let the reader understand then let those who are in Judea flee to the mountains."* (Matthew 24:15-16)

From these two examples we can see that some prophecies have more than one fulfillment. Keeping that in mind when we compare 1

Chronicles17:10-14 with 2 Samuel 7:11-14 we get a slightly different view of what was said.

> *"I declare to you that the LORD will build a house for you: When your days are over and you go to be with your fathers, I will raise up your offspring to succeed you, one of your own sons, and I will establish his kingdom. He is the one who will build a house for me, and I will establish his throne forever. I will be his father, and he will be my son. I will never take my love away from him, as I took it away from your predecessor. I will set him over my house and my kingdom forever; his throne will be established forever."* (1 Chronicles 17:10-14)

The first two sentences of both verses are somewhat the same in that God was going to build or establish a house for David, and after David had died, one of his offspring would rise up and God would establish his kingdom. Here is where the duel fulfillment starts to take place in that both Solomon and Jesus were considered David's offspring and both had their kingdoms established. But then we have a slight change in that both Solomon and Jesus will build a house for God, one being a shadow of the one to come, and that Solomon's throne was not established forever. Nowhere in scripture does it ever say that God referred to Solomon as His son, or that he would be set over God's kingdom. The Davidic sovereign kingdom ended in 587 BC with the fall of Jerusalem, and only Jesus was referred to as God's Son and only Jesus ever referred to God as His Father. It is clear that the last two sentences only find their true fulfillment in Jesus. The main fulfillment of these scriptures was not made through Solomon but through Jesus. Solomon's fulfillment was only a shadow of what was still to come. In the same way, the physical temple that Solomon built, with all its grandeur, was only a reflection of the spiritual one that was yet to come. *"They serve at a sanctuary that is a copy and shadow of what is in heaven." (Hebrews 8:5)*

When God spoke to David in 1 Chronicles 17:10 *"I declare to you that the LORD will build a house for you:"* we look to the obvious as "house" meaning lineage, because there was no recorded documentation of God building a dwelling place for David. But what if a dwelling place was exactly what God meant when He used the term "house"? When David had the desire to build God a house, he had in mind a place where God would dwell, and he could go and be in communion with Him. It was David's heart to always be there as well. *"Surely goodness and love will follow me all the days of my life, and I will dwell in the house of the LORD forever."* (Psalm 23:6) I believe this was God's plan all along, to create a place where God and man could be in communion together as it had been in the "garden".

Jesus made reference to the many ways He and the Father were in total communion, and they were never out of sync with each other. *"I tell you the truth, the Son can do nothing by himself; he can do only what he sees his Father doing, because whatever the Father does the Son also does."* (John 5:19) *"I and the Father are one."* (John 10:30)

What was it that made Jesus so in sync with the Father that He could say that they were one? Did he mean that they were such good friends that they knew each other very well and because of this they could anticipate each others moves? Or was it that they had the same heartfelt desires for mankind and that alone was enough for them to move in the same direction? Or were He the Father here on earth in a man's suit of flesh? Or when He said that He and the Father were one, was He referring to the fact that He and the Father were intrinsically linked heart and mind together and that He chose not do anything outside of the Father's will? Let's remember that Jesus was a man born of flesh and blood. If you were to cut Him He would have bled red blood. He was making these statements from His position as a human being. Even as a child Jesus had integral knowledge of the connection He had to the Father as shown when at the age of twelve He was found after three days in the temple having a discourse on the scriptures with the teachers of the law, and His response when found by His human parents was *"Did you not know that I had to be in my Father's house."* (Luke 2:40)

How was Jesus aware even as a child of the connection He had with the Father? What was the integral key that linked the human boy Jesus to the Father even at the age of twelve? There can be only be one answer to that question: the Holy Spirit. Let us not forget what the angel said to Mary. *"The Holy Spirit will come upon you, and the power of the Most High will overshadow you. So the holy one to be born will be called the Son of God."* (Luke 1:35) The Holy Spirit was upon Jesus from the point of conception and for the first thirty years of his life. We seem to have this idea that because nothing was recorded of Jesus' early years that He led a normal life and nothing out of the ordinary happened around Him. I am not so sure of this, for Mary His mother had an expectation of the abilities that Jesus had when they were at a wedding in Cana.

"On the third day a wedding took place at Cana in Galilee. Jesus' mother was there, and Jesus and his disciples had also been invited to the wedding. When the wine was gone, Jesus' mother said to him, "They have no more wine." "Dear woman, why do you involve me?" Jesus replied, "My time has not yet come." His mother said to the servants, "Do whatever he tells you." (John 2:1-5)

Do whatever He tells you, does not sound like a statement coming from one who had never seen the miraculous happen at the hands of Jesus. It sounds like a statement from one who might have seen her pots not run out of food even when there was not enough food to put into them!

So what is the difference between the time of His private upbringing and this public demonstration of the power of God within Jesus? We find the answer in Luke 3:21-22: the meeting of John the Baptist and Jesus at the Jordon River. It was here that the humanity of Jesus had its completion (Matthew 3:13) and the Holy Spirit moved from being upon Him to indwelling Him. He became the *"temple of the Holy Spirit"* and the glory of the Lord filled the temple.

"Jesus answered them, "Destroy this temple, and I will raise it again in three days." The Jews replied, "It has taken forty-six years to build this temple, and you are going to raise it in three days?" But the temple he had spoken of was his body. (John 2:19-21)

"The LORD declares to you that the LORD himself will establish a house for you. When your days are over and you rest with your fathers, I will raise up your offspring to succeed you, who will come from your own body, and I will establish his kingdom. He is the one who will build a house for my Name, and I will establish the throne of his kingdom forever. I will be his father, and he will be my son." (2 Samuel 7:11-13)

On the day that Jesus was baptized by John, this promise that God made to David was fulfilled. But in order for the rest of humanity to be able to enter into this temple, the law of the old covenant (Gen 15) had to be fulfilled and a new covenant made. (Jeremiah 21, Luke 22)

"It was now about the sixth hour, and darkness came over the whole

land until the ninth hour, for the sun stopped shining. And the curtain of the temple was torn in two. Jesus called out with a loud voice, "Father, into your hands I commit my spirit." When he had said this, he breathed his last." (Luke 23:44-46)

"When Christ came as high priest of the good things that are already here, he went through the greater and more perfect tabernacle that is not man-made." "He did not enter by means of the blood of goats and calves; but he entered the Most Holy Place once for all by his own blood, having obtained eternal redemption." "So Christ was sacrificed once to take away the sins of many people" (Hebrews 9:11-12, 28)

The sacrifice of the Lamb of God was a twofold sacrifice. Not only did it fulfill the old covenant demands, but like the old covenant (Gen 15:9-21), the new covenant required a sacrifice as well. (see appendix)

"Having given thanks, he broke it and said, this is my body, broken for you. Do this to remember me. After supper, he did the same thing with

the cup: This cup is my blood, my new covenant with you. Each time you drink this cup, remember me." (1 Corinthians 11:24-25 The Message)

To his disciples this action had a great impact later on after the resurrection for they understood the significance of a covenant meal. They understood how if there was to be a covenant, the eating of a covenant meal that was made of the covenant sacrifice (the Lamb of God) and the mixing of blood had to take place. But this is a whole other story for a different book. The point is that a new covenant was made between God and the man Jesus on behalf of all mankind, and by receiving the cleansing of our sins through the outpouring of His blood; we enter into this new covenant through our Mediator the Lord Jesus Christ. And how do we receive this cleansing of sins? By simply acknowledging from our heart that Jesus is the Son of God like He said He was, that we are a sinner just like everyone else is, and asking Jesus to forgive us and cleanse us from our sins. This is an act of faith that may or may not be accompanied by sensations of emotions, but it is guaranteed that once we do this our lives will no longer be the same.

In the same way that Jesus' body was the temple of the Holy Spirit, so our bodies become holy vessels for the Holy Spirit to indwell when we receive the cleansing power of the blood of Jesus. *"Don't you know that you yourselves are God's temple and that God's Spirit lives in you?"* (1 Corinthians 3:16) The early church experienced this at Pentecost when the Holy Spirit descended on them like tongues of fire. I believe that God manifested His glory in the form of fire at this moment so that there would be no doubt as to what was happening. Those who saw it would unquestionably know Who's presence they were in, as God used fire as a means of manifesting His presence all throughout the old testament. *"For the LORD your God is a consuming fire."* (Deuteronomy 4:24) God created a temple not made with human hands, a place where man can dwell together with his Creator, and enter into His presence at any time. Andrew Murray put it like this:

> "He has prepared for you an abiding dwelling with himself, where your whole life and every moment of it might be spent and where the work of your daily life might be done as you enjoy unbroken communion with him."

How do we know if the Spirit of God is within us? How do we come to the place of being in communion with God like Andrew Murray described? Quite simply like this: we ask the Holy Spirit to come in and dwell within our heart, and then believe that He will. *"If you then, though you are evil, know how to give good gifts to your children, how much more will your Father in heaven give the Holy Spirit to those who ask him!"* (Luke 11:13) It is not based upon the fact that we are good, or that we are more spiritual then the next, but it is based on the fact that God does not lie. When He says He will give us the Holy Spirit if we ask, He will. After we have asked Him to fill us with the Holy Spirit, we ask Him to reveal Himself to us and help us to know His voice. Ask and we will receive. Knock and the door will open to us. This is a matter of faith, a matter of looking at things that can not be seen as if we can.

So what about when the church comes together in one place? Are we then just a bunch of little temples running around in one building? *"So this is what the Sovereign LORD says: "See, I lay a stone in Zion, a tested stone, a precious cornerstone for a sure foundation."* (Isaiah 28:16) *"You also, like living stones, are being built into a spiritual house."* (1Peter 2:5)

It is my firm belief, as well as that of many others, that when we come together as one in His name, we are the house that God promised to build David in 1 Chronicles 17 and Jesus is the center piece, the foundation, the cornerstone of that house, the place where we should expect the physical manifestation of God's presence to appear.

The reality is that the Church is supposed to be a physical structure, a structure that houses the glory of the Living God; not a structure that is made with stone and brick, but a living structure made with precious living stones: *"you also, like living stones, are being built into a spiritual house"* (1Peter 2:5); a living structure that has a cornerstone that has been placed there by God Himself. Jesus said that when *"two or three come together in My name, there am I with them."* (Matthew 18:20) Either He is with us for real or He was just pulling our leg. The problem is that we have lost the expectation and realization that God's presence both spiritually and physically is here with us, both personally and collectively.

> "Having the reality of God's presence is not dependent on our being in a particular circumstance or place, but is only dependent on our determination to keep the Lord before us continually. Our problems arise when we refuse to place our trust in the reality of His presence."
> (Oswald Chambers)

When we gather in His name, the temple, the Holy Sanctuary of God, is manifested in the physical, and the Lamb of God is and will be there. Why? Because He said so. *"If two or three come together in my name, there am I with them."* Instead of taking Him at His word because we don't see Him, or feel Him in the manner in which we are accustomed to, we act like Thomas did and say that unless I see Him and touch Him I will not believe that He is here.

If we just go "to church" and have the attitude that the church is a designated place where we meet for fellowship, or have our spirits uplifted, we will have the tendency not to be disappointed if God does not show up. We sing our songs about God and what He has done in the past for one another, the preacher gives an encouraging word that gives us inspiration, and we leave feeling uplifted.

If we were to come "to church" with the attitude that we were gathering together to be a structure to house the manifested presence of God, we would not just leave feeling uplifted, but we would never want to leave. If we were to come with the attitude that when we gather we come together to pour out our love on the One who loves us most, I guarantee He will be there. It has always been His plan to commune with man, but we have a tendency to want things on our terms: "God You can show up, but we want a show, we want the wow factor, and You have to be done by 12 noon". The problem with this is that God does not go by our schedule and signs and wonders were never meant for the Church, but were meant as a sign for the unbeliever to confirm that God is real. If we, the Church were to have an expectation that the Head of the Church (Christ) was going to be right in the midst of us as He said He would be, the Sunday roast would be burnt, and the football games would go unwatched (or at least taped), and we would never have an empty seat, or room to even stand, for His very presence draws all men to Himself. We would not have to worry about healing the sick or seeing miracles happen; they would be happening right amongst us, and we would not even notice until after the fact.

Now that we have come to the understanding that we are a part of the temple of God, we now need to start living like it. Do we realize that God wants to commune with us at home, at work, at school, at play? The Holy Spirit is our teacher, helper, and guide, as well as comforter. And He is the same in us as He was in Jesus: our link to the Father. We have the freedom now to come into the presence of the Father whenever we want. We don't learn to do this over night, but we should strive to be in communion with God's presence all the time, where we are continually reliant on God to help us throughout the day. We speak to Him and He speaks to us, and we should have an expectation of His presence manifesting to our spirit. God wants to be involved in our everyday dealings, for wherever we are; there is His temple, and His glory.

"There are times when you choose to believe something that would normally be considered absolutely irrational. It doesn't mean that it is actually irrational, but it is surely not rational. Perhaps there is super-rationality; reason beyond the normal definitions of fact or database logic; something that only makes sense if you can see a bigger picture of reality. Maybe that is where faith fits in." (William P. Young)

CHAPTER THREE

A Life of Service; A Life of Worship

So where do we go from here? We have come to understand that we were designed and consecrated, thanks to Jesus's sacrifice on the cross, to be a house for the Holy Spirit to indwell, and that He wants to be a part of our everyday lives. So how should this look?

The best example is Jesus Himself. Jesus was constantly bombarded with the urgency of other people's lives, and yet He was never anxious about anything. The cares of this world were in His face continually yet He strived for nothing. Man's plans to make Him king of Judea, did not sway Him from the goal He had

35

set in front of Himself. Why? He, as a human being, had nothing more available to Him than we have today and yet He walked in this life as if everything were all prearranged for Him, and He was just along for the ride. What gives?

What gives is that Jesus from a little child cultivated an intimate relationship with the Father to the point that the two were inseparable. *"Anyone who has seen me has seen the Father."* (John 14:9) Jesus knew that His public life could only be a reflection of His private life, and that it was the intimacy that He had with the Father that enabled Him be who He was. But it was even more than that. Jesus knew the One who was guiding Him, who was giving Him the words to speak and who was doing the miracles that took place all around Him. *"The words I say to you are not just my own. Rather, it is the Father, living in me, who is doing his work."* (John 14:10)

How did Jesus cultivate this deep relationship with the Father? Simply, He spent time getting to know Him, and learned to trust Him. We get the idea that as soon as Jesus was born, He had this miraculous incredibly rich relationship with His heavenly Father. I don't think so. Yes, He would have known that He had a divine purpose and that His life was not an ordinary life, but He would have had to spend time listening to Mary and Joseph tell Him the stories of how He was conceived and what the angels had said about Him, as well as spend time learning what the scriptures said about Him. Then He would have had to make a decision to believe what was said about Himself.

He would have had to choose to listen to the guiding voice of the Holy Spirit, and He would have had to choose to go against what the world said and choose to follow His heavenly Father. What makes the story of Jesus so incredible is the fact the Jesus had the ability not to believe, not to spend time in the scriptures, not to spend time learning to listen to His Fathers voice, but He chose to. We also must follow the same path and choose to learn to recognize the Spirit's voice, choose to believe what the scriptures say, and choose to get to know our heavenly Father, just as Jesus did.

I have good news for you: God wants to make it easy for you to come to the place of intimacy with Him, but you have to take the first step, and that is to believe God wants this intimacy. Once you choose to believe this, ask Him to reveal Himself to you, in a new fresh way. I remember as a young Christian going for walks and feeling His hand in mine, having Him ask me to do things like kneel down in a park full of people and lift my hands in worship to Him in order to break the pride in my heart, and afterwards feeling His warm embrace. It is a matter of choice and no matter what the circumstance say, you have the power to believe. The more you choose to believe Him the more trust you will have that He will not let you down. God will not ask you to do something and then not empower you to do it.

At the heart of any relationship is communication. We communicate with one another through words, actions, and looks, but we cannot read each others thoughts. This is where the difference lies between the relationships we have with one another and that which we have with God. God speaks to us through our thoughts, and occasionally through our inner ear, where we hear God speaking to us in our own language, but it is mostly within our thoughts and impressions that God speaks to us. We get the impression that when God speaks to us it has to be this great big voice coming out of a cloud with bolts of lighting for added effect, but sorry to disappoint you, that's just not the case. I think that is why so many people who call themselves believers have never recognized God's voice speaking to them, for they are looking for this great "shazam" to happen when He does.

> *"Then a great and powerful wind tore the mountains apart and shattered the rocks before the LORD, but the*

LORD was not in the wind. After the wind there was an earthquake, but the LORD was not in the earthquake. After the earthquake came a fire, but the LORD was not in the fire. And after the fire came a gentle whisper. When Elijah heard it, he pulled his cloak over his face and went out and stood at the mouth of the cave. Then a voice said to him, "What are you doing here, Elijah?" (1 Kings 19:11-13)

It's that gentle little whisper deep within our soul, which we seem to just put off as our own thoughts, that is really God's Spirit talking to us. A monk called Brother Lawrence, who lived in France in the 1600's, put it like this "One should realize that this conversation with God occurs in the depth and center of the soul. It is there that the soul speaks to God heart to heart and always dwells in a great and profound peace that the soul enjoys in God."

It takes time in recognizing Gods voice from our own thoughts, time spent in His presence where we simply are quiet before God, while accepting the fact that He is with us. To start, just talk to Him as if He were standing in front of you, and with an expectation of His response. I remember as a young Christian I was so hungry to know God's voice that I would ask Him to guide me to where I had to go, and He would. Sometimes as I would be driving I would ask Him this and a thought would come to me accompanied by His loving inner peace, turn here and then there and the next thing you knew, I was where I needed to be. Other times I would ask and nothing would happen like before and I would resort to a map, but I would find my way to where I had to go. Does this mean God was not guiding me? I don't think so. I believe God answered my prayer in the form of the map book and opened my eyes to a quick and efficient route. God does not always speak to us in the same manner every time, but He will answer us, and when He does, His peace will be there. *"Then you will experience God's peace, which exceeds anything we can understand. His peace will guard your hearts and minds as you live in Christ Jesus."* (Philippians 4:7 NLT)

> "The actual presence of God, which includes any and all kinds of communion a person who still dwells on the earth, can possibly have with God in heaven. At times, he can live as if no one else existed on earth but himself and God. He lovingly speaks with God wherever he goes, asking Him for all he needs and rejoicing

with Him in a thousand ways. The trouble that happens in the world can become like a blaze of straw that goes out even as it catches fire, while the soul retains its interior peace in God." (Brother Lawrence)

We do not walk by feelings and emotions, but by faith, and just because we do not always feel His presence does not mean He is not present, but one who is guided by God will have His peace within. *"You will keep in perfect peace him whose mind is steadfast, because he trusts in you. Trust in the LORD forever, for the LORD, the LORD, is the Rock eternal."* (Isaiah 26:3-4)

God is not just interested in the big important things; He is interested in the little things as well. He wants to be a part of our everyday life, our home life, our work places, and our lives as we live with one another. As we begin to recognize the different ways in which God speaks to us, we will become more aware of His presence in our everyday life. I have come to rely on His wisdom so much when I work, that a lot of the most important events in my life have God's hands all over them. I remember once we were doing a conference in a 10,000 seat sports arena, in the former Yugoslavia and the echo was so bad we could not understand what was being said. I asked God to give me the wisdom on how to overcome this, and He did. Within a few hours I had the stadium sounding like a concert hall instead of the echo chamber it was. The thoughts just came to my mind and He brought back an article I had read on surround sound for concerts, and the plan of how to rid myself of this echo played out in my mind.

It is my firm belief that the wisdom that births the great inventions that are produced by men is inspired by God. I once met a man who invented a new form of motor that ran on hydrogen, and when asked about how he came up with the idea, he claimed the idea came to him in a vision while he was reading the Bible. Coincidence? I dont think so, but more like God conveying wisdom to him in the form of a vision and giving understanding in what to do with it.

> *"Then the LORD said to Moses, "See, I have chosen Bezalel son of Uri, the son of Hur, of the tribe of Judah, and I have filled him with the Spirit of God, with skill, ability and knowledge in all kinds of crafts to make artistic designs for work in gold, silver and bronze, to cut and set stones, to work in wood, and to engage in all kinds of craftsmanship."*
> (Exodus 31:1-5)

God wants to be involved in every aspect of our lives, from the decisons we make to what we do with our time. It is not that God is going to stand there and tell us what to do all day long; we have our own free will upon which God will never intrude, but if we invite Him to guide us in our decisions and planning and are willing to be obediant to what He shows us, we will never have to worry about whether we are in His will or not, or if we are making a wrong choice.

If Christians would just submit their decision-making process to Jesus, they would avoid finding themselves in a wrong marriage, or a wrong career, etc. We have to remember that we have the same access to God that Jesus had. (Brennan Manning)

We also have to remember that just because we are doing what God is directing us to do, does not mean that everything will be easy or turn out the way we think it should. But we can always rest in the knowledge that God's presence and His peace will be with us, and His purposes will be accomplished. The sum of Jesus's free will choice to be obedient to the Father's leading was captured in the Garden of Gethsemane when Jesus spoke these words, *"My Father, if it is possible, may this cup be taken from me. Yet not as I will, but as you will."* (Matthew 26:39) Obedience to God's leading will not only affect you, but every one around you as well; don't be surprised if your fellow believers are not too keen on your path, for it will more than likely at some point interfere with their plans for you. Jesus' determination to complete His journey to the cross, flew in the face of many of His followers who were just as determined to make Him king over Israel. In the end they left Him and He walked the last part of His journey alone, thus finishing what His Father had started.

Jesus, while He walked the path that God had led Him on, never once complained about it; He just expected that God had allowed the circumstance to be what they were. He was content in the plan that God had for Him and was not concerned with the proverbial "climbing the ladder". So what made Him so content in his position in life? Jesus was a homeless man (Matthew 8:20), and although He had the means of providing for himself with His skills in carpentry, which would have been taught to him by Joseph, He never tried to make ends meet by going outside of God's plan. What was it that made Him so free from the demands of this world, and gave Him the ability to never give any consideration to His own well being? The answer can only be love. Jesus loved the Father with all His heart, all His might, and all His being, and loved the people around Him as Himself, so that everything He did was based on that. It was the love He had for the Father and the knowledge of how much the Father loved Him that kept Him from veering from the objective, and gave Him the empowerment to love others as Himself, even when they spat right in His face.

"Be imitators of God, therefore, as dearly loved children and live a life of love, just as Christ loved us and gave himself up for us as a fragrant offering and sacrifice to God" (Ephesians 5:1-2) This is not an easy task, and cannot be done by sheer willpower, but can only be accomplished by remaining in the presence of God, and allowing Him to pour His love through us. The more we choose to surrender our will to the power of God's love, the more His presence fills us. After all, we must remember that love is not a feeling, nor an emotion, but true love is a choice, a choice that has powerful effects, but nevertheless, a choice. One step at a time, choosing to surrender the response of our will to that of love will produce all the benefits of love (i.e. feelings), but if we wait for those feelings to guide us in our choices, we will never choose love, but our own self interest every time.

The motive behind every action that Jesus undertook was love, first for the Father, then for His fellow man. Great or small, His motive was love. When he turned water into wine, or healed the sick, when He turned over the tables in the temple, or walked down the Via Dolorosa to Calvary, His motive for these actions was love.

"The pettiness of the deed would not diminish the worth of the offering, because God, needing nothing, considers in our works only the love that accompanies them." (Joseph de Beaufort) Being obedient to the direction of God is meaningless if it is not motivated by love. No matter what we do for God, big or small unless it is birthed from love, it will be of no reward.

"Therefore, I urge you, brothers, in view of God's mercy, to offer your bodies as living sacrifices, holy and pleasing to God, this is your spiritual act of worship." (Romans 12:1) When we choose, motivated by the love we have for Him, to set aside our plans, our desires, and even our own natural talents, and choose to allow God to direct us as He wishes; our lives become a fragrant offering and sacrifice to God, which is an act of worship. After all, worship is a living, active expression of our love for Him, and we were designed to worship Him. No matter if we are at work, at play, at home, or at church (which is an oxymoron, for if we *are* the church how can we be *at* church?) our lives should be an act of worship to God. Be it a great thing or a small thing, a life lived out of the love we have for Him, is a life lived with worship as a lifestyle, birthed out of being in the intimate presence of God.

Now the trick is to remain in that attitude of worship! It is easy to be motivated by love when everything is going well and we have time to prepare a response to things that are not to our liking. But when things blindside us, and injustice comes at us out of nowhere, choosing to act in love is a near impossible thing. This is where the grace of God comes into play, and although our first reaction may not have been a gesture of love, God will empower us to choose not to remain there but to move into an attitude of love. It is amazing how anger and bitterness flee, when we start to pray blessings on the person that just cut us off in traffic. The choice is ours. God will not force us to act in love, but as soon as we choose to, He empowers us with His love. The quicker we choose, the less time it takes to move back into an attitude of worship, until this becomes almost seamless.

So when those times of trials arise and catch us off guard (and they will) and our attitude is not of a loving worshipful nature, lets not get exasperated by our attitude. Instead let's choose to act in love. One of the greatest acts of worship is when, motivated by God's love, we ask someone to forgive us for the way we acted, when they were the ones who initiated the problem to begin with. A lifestyle of worship is not easy, but outside of accepting Jesus as our Savior, it is the most rewarding choice one can make here on earth.

Chapter Four

Music: An Audible Part Of Our Worship

"It is good to praise the LORD and make music to your name, O Most High, to proclaim your love in the morning and your faithfulness at night, to the music of the ten-stringed lyre and the melody of the harp." (Psalm 92:13)

"And let us consider how we may spur one another on toward love and good deeds. Let us not give up meeting together, as some are in the

habit of doing, but let us encourage
one another." (Hebrews 10:24-25)

In the previous chapter we have discussed an idea of a life style of worship, in this chapter we will look at an audible part of worship, music.

After the first century of the birth of the church, both the public praising and worshiping of God through music, and the edifying and building up of one another was laid aside and replaced with the teaching of doctrines. There was such an uproar over the different doctrines that were springing up that divisions within the church had become prominent, and the loving actions of worship were all but lost in the church. By the time the fourth century had passed, what was known as the "Church" had moved from being known for its love for God, to being a religious organization known for its thirst for power and political domination. However, there was a remnant of true worshipers of God that still existed in the church, and they kept the true passion of the church alive during those times of darkness.

For close to 1500 years the corporate singing of songs to God within church gatherings was all but lost until the reformers reintroduced the singing of psalms and hymns in their meetings. Funny how it is that when we started to corporately sing to God again, revivals started to break forth. People were hungry to shed the dead traditions of the church and get back to the real purpose of the church, which is to testify of His glory and His love.

In the 18th and 19th century we saw a move from doctrinal preaching to reading of the Bible publicly and ministering to the people. The Bible as we know it today was available to the public at large and a hunger for God within the church was growing which had not been seen since the days of the book of Acts. In 1727 revival broke out in what we call Germany today that would eventually affect the whole western world. This was known as the "First Great Awakening." From that period on until the first part of the twentieth century waves of revivals were flooding across the world, in which God's Spirit was being poured out upon His people. His manifested presence was prevalent in the meetings that took place in which people were being reported to being filled with God's Spirit. It was in 1904; in Wales that the last wave of the "Great Awakenings" started that would eventually spread to Los Angles and Azusa Street where the birth of what we call the Pentecostal movement was born.

Out of these great world wide awakenings, songs and hymns were written that would be the basis of the music that would be sung in those services. From such composers of the awakened Church like John Newton and Johann Bach, of the 18th century and Fanny Crosby and William Booth of the 19th century, new songs of the heart were penned as offerings to God and these songs still influence us today. They portrayed the passion and zeal that was being implanted in the hearts of the people of that time and one key factor to this new music was that it was in keeping with the musical genre of that day, a genre that the average person coming into the church could relate to.

As time changed the face of how the church looked changed, as did it's music, but one thing stayed the same in church music: from the early 1700's to end of the 1920's the music of the church was written with the express purpose of being sung in church services, and to ministered only it those in attendance.

The next 40 years produced small pockets of renewals and new songs were being written but not on the scale of the past 220 years, and their effects were not felt world wide.

Then in the late 1960s with the Jesus People movement, we started to see arise a world-wide passion for an intimate relationship with God, and the songs that were sung in church started to take on a more personal theme again. It was around this time that the division around the style of music that was played in church (which actually started in Bach's time) intensified. People who went to church because "that's what good people do" were being confronted with shabbily dressed, long haired people sitting in their favorite pews, and the passion coming from the hearts of these "Jesus Freaks" was causing them to look very deep into their own lives and hearts.

There was one major difference in this awakening from the one of the previous two centuries. All of the other awakenings that happened were birthed out of heart-wrenched prayer meetings, in which individuals poured out their hearts to God in intercession asking God to move. There was no one prayer meeting, or tent meeting that started it, but individuals were sensing that God was getting ready to do something and were praying for God to fulfill whatever that was. People started to come to know God outside the church in the midst of everyday life and then came into the church to find out what to do next. God was also using music to draw the people to Himself, and God was also moving through the music of the day speaking to the hearts of many people, drawing them to Himself. He used Christians in the music industry to reach other musicians and their music then took on a very Christian theme.

Out of this was birthed an extraordinary hunger for God within the church, and a desire to move past the comfortable and into the heat of His passion that comes from His presence.

Miracles started to be a normal part of church again, and the gifts of the Spirit were evident in most denominations. Out of this came a resurgence of one of the reasons why we gather together and the church as a whole started to regain its focus to encourage and edify one another to good works of love. The music we sang and listened to portrayed this and ministering to one another became the main focus of church gatherings. Our songs were about what God has done for us, or about how we were to overcome every obstacle. It was not until the beginning of the twenty-first century that we saw a change in the direction of our songs. God began to stir up His church again, and draw us back to Himself. Our music again portrayed this shift as it took on a focus of worship <u>to</u> Him instead of just singing <u>about</u> Him. Yet a continuing division over musical style and the instruments that are used still hinders the Church as a whole, from experiencing total unity in worship.

Right from the start, when the Reformers reintroduced singing in the meetings, this division over music in the church was on, and has been an area of contention ever since: what should be allowed to be sung, what instruments, if any, should be allowed, and what about those drums!!!! Some would say that this contention really only started back with the Jesus People Movement, and that they brought secular music into the church and corrupted the hearts and minds of our kids.

> "Secular music, do you say, belongs to the devil? Does it? Well, if it did I would plunder him for it, for he has no right to a single note of the whole seven. Every note, and every strain, and every harmony is divine, and belongs to us. So consecrate your voice and your instruments. Bring out your comets and harps and organs and flutes and violins and pianos and drums, and everything else that can make melody. Offer them to God, and use them to make all the hearts about you merry before the Lord." *"Why should the devil have all the best tunes?"* (William Booth, 1880, founder of the Salvation Army)

This division started when the Reformers of the 1700's finally began to sing praise and worship songs to God publicly again and it should not surprise us for after all, according to certain translations of Ezekiel 28:13 and Isaiah 14:11, Lucifer's (Satan's name before his fall) body was created by God to make music. Seeing that music was so dear to Him, Satan would stop at nothing to try and prevent us using our God-given talents as musicians and singers to praise and worship God with music. At the heart of this continuous controversy are man-made doctrines that are based on personal preference and religious rhetoric, which Satan uses to keep the church divided. *"If a house is divided against itself, that house cannot stand."* (Mark 3:25)

There are those who say it is a generational gap that is causing the problem, but that is just a lame excuse for not honoring and loving one another. I've been in worship services where the musicians were of every age group, the genre was of a fast upbeat contemporary format, and the older gray-haired people were leading the way with hands raised and voices flowing with praise. Then they would break into a worshipful hymn and the young people were just as infused as the older ones. The reason is simple. They were focused on the One to whom the songs where being sung, and not on the songs themselves.

When we look at scriptures as a reference to the way music should be used in church services, we can put away a lot of these misguided weapons that Satan uses to keep us divided. First and foremost, we must remember that everything we do must be centered in love, first to God and then to one another. (Did you notice I left self out?) Secondly, the Old Testament scriptures are relevant to us today as well, not that we are under the law, but rather they are for our example. *"For everything that was written in the past was written to teach us, so that through endurance and the encouragement of the Scriptures we might have hope."* (Romans 15:4)

Let us see what the scriptures say. The scriptures encourage musicians of all ages to take part, and not to just learn enough to get by but to be skilled in the instruments (vocals included) they are using. *"All of them trained and skilled in music for the LORD - they numbered 288. Young and old alike, teacher as well as student, cast lots for their duties."* (1 Chronicles 25:7-8). If we look at this as a model of what our worship teams should look like, we will eliminate a lot of the segregation that goes on in our churches. The idea that only young people can lead young people in worship, and vice versa is nonsense. It is a worldly way of looking at things. Too many people have been alienated in the past because of age, how they look, or their status in society. If people have a desire to learn and are applying effort to the principles of playing an instrument or singing, there should be room for them. The standard today is to push the teachers out and have only the students (young people) play, in order to attract younger people to our gatherings. If we were to honor all people equally, we would still attract the younger generation.

There is also an idea floating around that God only likes certain genres of music, and anything other than those particular genres is an abomination to Him, especially music that is beat oriented. But if we were to look to the scriptures, we would find no mention of any specific genre that is ordained for praising and worshiping God. What we will find is that whatever music is played should come from a heart full of passion. *"My heart is steadfast, O God; I will sing and make music with all my soul."* (Psalm 108:1) *"I will praise you, O LORD, with all my heart" "I will sing your praise."* (Psalm 138:1)

I know I haven't come up with a scripture that allows different music genres to be used, but I will guarantee that we will not find one that gives restrictions.

As a matter of fact, King David instructed the music of Psalm 8 to be played on a Philistine lute (a pear shaped guitar like instrument) set to a particular Hittite tune. Some of the best hymns we sing today like "Oh, the Blood of Jesus" from the 1880's were set to a music style that the general population of that day was able to relate to it in order to covey the message that was coming from the writer's heart.

Music is a means of emotional expression to convey a message, and the genre is dependent on the culture that the writer is from and is influenced by. From the time when Moses was given the plans for the tabernacle to the time when Jesus walked the earth, the music of the Jewish culture was the same genre as that which was used in worship. When the fall of Jerusalem occurred and the church was dispersed throughout the known world, the culture that the people were from influenced the music they used to worship God with. If God had ordained only a certain genre, and only certain instruments, then we would be still using the Hebraic style of music and instruments of that time period to worship God with. After all, Jesus was of Jewish decent through Mary, and was born and raised in that Jewish culture.

One of the reasons that music style is such an issue in church meetings is because of personal preference, and the sentimental worshiping of memories invoked in us when we first sang or heard a song. Using personal preference as a means of dictating what is the right or wrong way to worship God is nothing more than pride, founded on the idea that only the genre of music that is tasteful to me personally is good enough for the Lord, and that anything other than this must be of the devil. "There is just no way I can worship God with this style of music," is a statement made from a heart of pride, for worship, like love, is a choice and we should never allow anything to stop us from worshiping God. *"Then my head will be exalted above the enemies who surround me; at his tabernacle will I sacrifice with shouts of joy; I will sing and make music to the LORD."* (Psalm 27:6) Different music genres will obviously draw us, just out of familiarity, and there is nothing wrong with having a preferred genre, but our personal preference should never dictate whether we can worship God or not through a different musical genre.

Any song, by any writer, in any genre, that is focused on pouring love out to God, should inspire us to do just that, and we should embrace all forms of music that do this.

And by the way, the "good old days" should be no different from today if we are allowing God to have His way in our lives. *"I will sing a new song to you, O God; on the ten-stringed lyre I will make music to you."* (Psalm 144:9) *"Praise the LORD. Sing to the LORD a new song, his praise in the assembly of the saints."* (Psalm 149:1)

It has also been stated that church music should be mostly quiet, relaxing, and meditative music. There is a place for this, but praise itself is an expressive verb. *"Come, let us sing for joy to the LORD; let us shout aloud to the Rock of our salvation. Let us come before him with thanksgiving and extol him with music and song."* (Psalm 95:1-2) This doesn't sound too quiet and relaxing to me! I like the way the Message translates it. *"Come, let's shout praises to God, raise the roof for the Rock who saved us! Let's march into his presence singing praises, lifting the rafters with our hymns!"* Both words "praise" and "worship" evoke emotions and passion in us that are exceedingly expressive, and the music should follow that same vein of expression. The music must also be played at a volume that suits that expression as well, for it is nearly impossible to get people to sing out loud if they drown out the ones who are leading them, or if they cannot hear themselves sing because the music is too loud. Having the right volume is critical in having people enter into worship; if they cannot follow the music, then we might as well be playing to ourselves.

There are five different types of music used within the church today: praise, worship, testimonial, doctrinal, and ministerial. These are divided into two categories: horizontal (human to human) and vertical (human to God). Testimonial, doctrinal, and ministerial music fall under the horizontal category, whereas praise and worship fall under the vertical category.

Horizontal music is needed within our church meetings, and is used to encourage one another in our walk, or our knowledge of God, *"I will sing of the Lord's great love forever; with my mouth I will make your faithfulness known through all generations."* (Psalm 89:1) but we must all ways remember that *it is not* praise or worship. A song, that is testimonial in nature like '*I Found Jesus*' by Martin Smith sings about our personal experiences and is encouraging and uplifting. A doctrinal song like, '*The Lord Is Gracious And Compassionate*' by Graham Ord will generally help solidify our understanding of scriptures and what we believe as a body. Whereas a type of song that is ministerial in nature like, '*There is Freedom*' by Mike Larson and Ben Cantelon are songs written with the sole purpose of drawing us close to God. All three of these types have the ability to cross over between the different uses, but they will always remain horizontal.

There is a time and a place for horizontal music within our gatherings, but the scriptures are clear that our music should be predominately towards God. In the scriptures we are encouraged to sing to one another only nine times, but we are encouraged to sing to God 58 times.

> *"Praise the LORD with the harp; make music to him on the ten-stringed lyre."* (Psalm 33:2)

> *"Praise the Lord, all you Gentiles, and sing praises to him, all you peoples."* (Romans 15:11)

*"I will sing to the LORD, I will sing;
I will make music to the LORD, the
God of Israel."* (Judges 5:3)

The majority of the hymns and choruses we sing are horizontal in nature, for they are written about God or salvation, and are designed to stir up our souls that we might be encouraged to walk on in the Lord. This is good, and is needed, but if the sole focus of our music, preaching, and our general time together is on encouraging and ministering to one another, we miss one of the greatest reasons we should gather together, which is to minister to God corporately. Jesus asked the Samaritan woman at the well to *"Give Me a drink"* (John 4:7). "How many of us are expecting Jesus Christ to quench our thirst when we should be satisfying Him!" (Oswald Chambers)

Think of it this way, if you have a person with whom you are in love with and who is in love with you, and while the one you love is standing right there with you, would you turn from that person whom you love, and only tell others around you and not that person, how much you love and appreciate that person? But that is exactly what we do when our music is mostly concentrated on singing about God to one another.

Vertical music is music that is designed and written to be sung and played directly to God, and this is where the spirit of man can intertwine with the Spirit of God. In order for one to fully take part in the singing of these songs, one must sing these songs from the heart.

> *"Yet a time is coming and has now come when the true worshipers will worship the Father in spirit and truth, for they are the kind of worshipers the Father seeks. God is spirit, and his worshipers must worship in spirit and in truth."* (John 4:23-24)

It is impossible to sing these songs <u>from the heart</u> without passion and emotion, and it is quite common to have times of corporate prayerful praise and worship, accompanied with the spiritual gift of prophecy, break forth in different forms (spoken, sung, or played on instruments) when singing these songs to God.

It is sometimes hard to tell when praise turns into worship, but Pastor Charlotte Baker describes it like this: "Praise, an operation of faith, is an instrument which will create the atmosphere for the presence of God. In contrast, worship is the expression of our response to His Presence." Prayer and the singing of vertical songs should be synonymous with one another, for after all, prayer is nothing more than communicating with God. Praise and worship (musically) are singing and playing songs to God which are both forms of communication. *"About midnight Paul and Silas were praying and singing hymns to God."* (Acts 16:25) An allegorical picture of this is found in Revelation 5:8;

> *"And when he had taken it, the four living creatures and the twenty-four elders fell down before the Lamb. Each one had a harp and they were holding golden bowls full of incense, which are the prayers of the saints."*

The act of falling down before God in the Old Testament was always an act of worship, and humility, the harp representing the music of worship. Whenever there was corporate worship of God, incense was burned to honor Him. In this picture, we see that the incense is our prayers.

> *"When Solomon finished praying, fire came down from heaven and consumed the burnt offering and the sacrifices, and the glory of the LORD filled the temple. The priests could not enter the temple of the LORD because the glory of the LORD filled it. When all the Israelites saw the fire*

coming down and the glory of the LORD above the temple, they knelt on the pavement with their faces to the ground, and they worshiped and gave thanks to the LORD, saying, "He is good; his love endures forever." (2 Chronicles 7:1-3)

The willingness to incorporate humility into our worship causes us to be intertwined with the Spirit of God. It may take the form of kneeling or bowing, or even dancing with all our might before Him, but in ether sense, humility is a sweet fragrance to God. It is an incredible experience when we lose ourselves in worship with our eyes closed, feeling impressed to kneel before our King and when we open our eyes again we find just about everyone else on their knees as well.

When we the Church set our focus on ministering to God first and to man second, we will find an atmosphere permeated with the manifested presence of God. It is out of this attitude of pouring out from the bottom of our souls unto God that creates the atmosphere for God to manifest Himself in our midst. It is in His manifested presence that people's lives are changed, the blind receive their sight, and diseases are healed, all without man's involvement. Signs and wonders occurred throughout Jesus' walk, a confirmation to the fact that the Kingdom of God was here with us. (Matthew 12:28). In the same sense God uses signs and wonders to confirm the very fact that the kingdom and the King are in our midst. Why? Because God is drawing all people to Himself, for we know that no man can come to Jesus unless the Father draws him. Since Jesus has been lifted up from the earth, He will draw all men to Himself. (John 6:44, John 12:32)

I have been in worship services where God's presence was unmistakable, and in the midst of the worship people were healed of the illness that plagued them. No man laid hands on them, or anointed them with oil; they weren't even looking for healing, they were just looking for Jesus. They found the One they were seeking and He met their needs personally. When we take the focus of our attention off ourselves and place it on God, God has a way of meeting us right where we are. *"Seek first his kingdom and his righteousness, and all these things will be given to you as well."* (Matthew 6:33)

I am not saying that if we worship God with all our heart and all our mind, we will have a life free of any difficulty or illness. No, not at all, but we will have a life that when hard times come, and they will, we will not have to walk alone through them. His presence will carry us and we will hardly notice them for we will be so focused on the object of our affection, that we pass through those times with little recognition of them. Signs and wonders are mostly meant for the nonbeliever as their purpose is to confirm Gods presence, whereas the presence of God is the life-blood of a person who knows God personally. Once we have tasted and been in His intimate manifested presence, we will be ruined to anything but that.

> *"Here I am! I stand at the door and knock. If anyone hears my voice and opens the door, I will come in and eat with him, and he with me."* (Revelation 3:20)

CHAPTER FIVE

People, Get Ready

When we think of an encounter with God, we normally think of signs and wonders as the evidence that verifies God is with us. In the past, this has been the case. When what we call a revival would take place, signs and wonders were the means by which God revealed Himself to His people. We call this an awakening or a revival, and rightly so, for the definitions of these titles are quite true, because up to that point we were either spiritually dead or at best, fast asleep to the aspects of God being in our midst.

When we are young in our walk with the Lord, signs and wonders thrill us, for we are not used to being in God's presence, but as we grow in our relationship with Him we realize that signs and wonders are God showing us His hand, covering Himself from us, leaving us with a sense of His presence, so that we will seek Him all the more. The problem is when we start to think that this is all God is willing to reveal to us and become quite satisfied with just that. Yet all along God has wanted to really be our friend, our best friend, a friend closer than a brother - our Father!

When we go to meetings only because there are signs and wonders happening, what we want and seek shows how little we know of God. This bids us to ask the question: are we really seeking God, or are we only interested in being thrilled by the show of God's power? Do not get me wrong, I am not saying that if we are thrilled about seeing signs and wonders we are not saved, or that we are less of a Christian, and that signs and wonders are "of the Devil". I am just simply stating that if we are chasing after signs and wonders, and spiritual goose bumps, so that we can feel good and alive, we are missing out on the very aspect of what God desires for us - His face!

> *"The LORD would speak to Moses face to face, as a man speaks with his friend."* (Exodus 33:11)

"Greater love has no one than this, that he lay down his life for his friends. You are my friends if you do what I command. I no longer call you servants, because a servant does not know his master's business. Instead, I have called you friends, for everything that I learned from my Father I have made known to you." (John 15:13-15)

We have had a few world-wide "awakenings" happen within the last twenty years where people, mostly Christians, were spiritually awakened again to the Holy Spirit, but these "awakenings" had very little impact on society as a whole and any lingering effects have all but worn off.

The last great move that came through our land that affected the society and the culture they lived in, was back in the late '60s and early '70s with the Jesus People Movement. At that time, people who did not have any means of knowing God came to know Him. It was His presence interjected into their lives that made the difference. It wasn't about an event or laying hands on people or a man demonstrating signs and wonders that brought these people to Christ; it was the fact that God's presence was interjected into their lives on a very intimate basis which brought them to the cross. Many of the people I knew from that era who came to know the Lord came to know Him by God revealing Himself to them through His presence. People where tired of the same old, same old, and were hungry for a change, so when God started to reveal Himself to people, it wasn't just in the churches. God was moving in the bars, in the parks, in the schools, in the work place, and God was using anything and everything to get their attention. Why? Because they were hungry for something more than a Sunday morning religion, something to be able to put their hope in. They didn't want to hear just stories about "back when"; they wanted to encounter the God that spoke to Moses face to face and hear Him speak with them.

Since that time, many of the things that we have seen within the church have been God's hand being revealed to those who were already in the church, kind of like a reminder of "Hey, I am still here, seek Me and you will find Me." Signs and wonders were never meant to be for the church, but were meant to be as a sign for unbelievers to let them know that God was alive and well. We have taken signs and wonders and turned them into a show for the church so that people can be entertained by the Almighty God. If you go to a lot of the services where signs and wonders flow freely, you will very rarely find one person who is not saved, but instead you find Christians who are coming to watch all the things happen around them or to them, and be entertained by God. They leave feeling refreshed and invigorated, but their lives are rarely changed and they remain the same old person, looking for their next spiritual fix.

The world is hungry for the supernatural; just look at all the television shows such as Ghost Whisperer, or Medium and other such shows that dedicate their criteria to the supernatural. New Age themes that used to be obscure are now everyday occurrences within society. Countless people read their "horror" scopes daily, just to get a touch of the supernatural in their lives. **People are hungry.**

The Church today is starting regain its hunger for God. Many of us are not satisfied with just seeing His hand move amongst us, or have Him touch us as He passes by. We want Him. We are not satisfied with just having Him touch us, to get our Holy Ghost goose bumps we want to have His presence with us 24 / 7. All the things around us that affect our flesh help us to know that God is near, but we are not satisfied with just having Jesus pass by. We want Him inside us and through us. Are we selfish? I don't think so. Many Christians including myself are tired of doing church. We're tired of hearing about how God moved in this country and that country. We want God here with us now! We're not satisfied with the same old status quo.

It is my firm conviction that there are three main reasons why we don't see a lot of signs and wonders on a regular basis in our church meetings today. Oh, we have the odd person healed or prophetic word given here and there but nothing like what we should have. The first reason is that we may not be always sure what God's will is in the matter, then we go and lay hands on people and pray, "If it is your will Lord please touch them, maybe".

The second reason is that we may attribute the signs and wonders, when they do happen; to the person God uses to perform them. How many times have we seen people that come up for prayer huddle around the special speaker, and not around any of the other people who may be there to pray for them as well. Thirdly and most importantly, signs and wonders were never meant to be show-cased in a church meeting.

If we pray for someone, and we ask, hoping that God hears us and is willing to answer our prayers, and when we don't see our prayers answered we chalk it up to the fact that the other person just didn't have enough faith. But the reality of the fact is that we are to pray with faith and without doubt. Faith only comes from hearing the word of God.

"So then faith cometh by hearing, and hearing by the word of God." (Romans 10:17 KJV),

"I tell you the truth, if you have faith and do not doubt, not only can you do what was done to the fig tree, but also you can say to this mountain, 'Go, throw yourself into the sea,' and it will be done." (Matthew 21:21).

If we are not listening to what God says to us by His Spirit how can we have the faith to pray effectively? This can only come from having a life disciplined in waiting and listening to the One who knows what the real issue is, so that when we pray, we pray in faith according to what He says to us, and not according to our own understanding.

"So whatever I say is just what the Father has told me to say." (John 12:50) Faith comes from hearing from God and believing in what He says.

Many times I have gone to pray for someone, but when I wait until God speaks to my heart on the matter, I end up praying something totally different than what I intended to pray. When we pray according to His direction this will sometimes not sit well with those around us, for God does not mess around and goes for the root of the problem, not just the symptoms. This can occasionally get messy, yet the end result is that the problem is addressed. Sometimes He will deal with other things first before getting to the problem. The question is, are we ready to walk by faith when we pray for people? If we are, we will see results, but they just may not be the ones we were expecting.

Now when we do see signs and wonders happening we have a tendency to attribute them to the person whom God uses to perform them through. So many times we see people moving in signs and wonders and everyone is so mesmerized by them that they don't recognize that these people are no different from you and me and have no power of their own. It is God who is behind the signs and wonders. If they are operating in the gifts of the Holy Spirit, they are operating in a power that is not their own. People, in a lot of cases, have a tendency to put those who God uses on pedestals and idolize them. Sadly, some who are put on these pedestals do not discourage this type of behavior because it helps to bring in the money and gives them the notoriety they seek.

Just because people operate in signs and wonders does not mean that they have a close relationship with God, or that their lives are in order. Just look at the long list of fallen TV evangelists that right up until they were exposed were performing signs and wonders regularly.

Why were they able to do this, you ask? The answer is quite simple; God does not take back His gifts. They were operating in the gift of miracles which they received while they were still close to God. *"for God's gifts and his call are irrevocable"* (Romans 11:29). They believed in the gifting, and that God had placed it upon them. Their faith was in the gifting, and they continued to pray without doubting, thus the miracles. It is my firm belief that these men fell away because they lost their dependence on the One who gave the gift, and grew comfortable moving in the gift on their own.

> "Not everyone who says to me, 'Lord, Lord,' will enter the kingdom of heaven, but only the one who does the will of my Father who is in heaven. Many will say to me on that day, 'Lord, Lord, did we not prophesy in your name and in your name drive out demons and in your name perform many miracles?' Then I will tell them plainly, 'I never knew you. Away from me, you evildoers!'"
> (Matthew 7:21-23)

Signs and wonders are meant to be operating in every believer, but only under the influence and direction of the Holy Spirit. When we acknowledge God as the Author and Performer of the signs, and not ourselves, we make it easier to squash the religious pride in our lives, and move unhampered by selfish motives.

The third reason why signs and wonders are not prevalent in our Church services is due to the fact that signs and wonders were never meant to be show-cased in our meetings. Signs and wonders are meant to be a sign to those who do not know Him, to prove that God is present. We have the idea that God only works through certain special people and that it has to be just the right environment for signs and wonders to be performed. The fact is that if we are in tune to what God is doing around us, as we are obedient to what God shows us, signs and wonders will follow us wherever we are. They just may not be the big flashy miracles, but never the less, signs to the unbeliever that God is with us. One of the greatest signs is God's tangible presence. Healings can be disputed, prophesies can be misunderstood, but when someone comes face to face with the tangible presence of God, it will leave a mark on their lives that will last forever! The question remains though, are we ready to be a fool for Christ? Are we ready to pray for someone right in the middle of the street when God prompts us to? Are we ready to go up to a stranger who is distraught and give them a solution to their problem when God shows us their predicament and what to do about it? Are we ready to have God invade our lives outside of "Church", and give account to those around us as to what is happening?

A friend of mine told me of one of these encounters when she started to share about her relationship with God at a jazz festival.

> "Our band was hired to go up to the Kelona Jazz Festival, in which we had three different gigs scheduled. It was the first time this bass player had worked with us and he was very open to what we were about and said he didn't know what was happening, but he knew something was happening. As the nights went on I was getting tired so I asked the Lord to make the difference up, to fill up the holes. I have a natural performance ability, but when you're tired and you are feeling physically worn out all that kind of fades. It was our last show, and we started to do our last set and I started to speak in between the songs about my relationship with the Lord and for allowing me to work in music with these people that He provided. I didn't talk in Christianize, I just spoke normal and this table starts

to say Amen which I thought it was really strange because this was a secular venue. At the break I found out they were Baptist people when they came forward and they were crying and hugging me, thanking me for they could sense the presence of the Lord. They said do you still go to church, and I said yes I am a Christian, and they said they could tell. The night went and there was a time near the end of the night I felt a distinct presence of the Holy Spirit there I just knew He had come, and I found out later that the bass player said to the piano player "what the hell is that that happened" he said "that something happened, something was here", and the piano player said" well you know that Glenda's dad is a Pastor and she is kinda like a shaman." I was so thankful you know, I do believe that the Holy Spirit abides and when we ask him to come, He does. We don't need to coerce people who don't know Christ to come into some strange thing, because the Spirit can touch their life. It doesn't have to be something that is odd or scary to them, but its warm and it is pleasant. I found through out my life working in a secular environment if l act just how I am, there is all sorts of opportunities in different ways to share Christ or my experience with Christ." (Glenda Rae Wade)

"People get ready, there's a train comin' You don't need no baggage, you just get on board. All you need is faith to hear the diesels hummin'. You don't need no ticket you just thank the Lord." (Curtis Mayfield)

I believe God wants to bring a mighty move of His Spirit upon this earth, one that reaches into every level of society, where we see signs and wonders happening on a regular basis. I also believe this will not happen just within the church, but instead will happen within the marketplace. As the church regains even more of its hunger for the presence of God and stops trying to gain notoriety for itself, but instead adopts John the Baptist's position that "I must become less and He must become more", we will see God move among us like He did with the apostles. When they moved and did things, it was not under their own understanding, but under the influence of the Holy Spirit, (Act 8,

10) and they had an expectation that God would move among them.

A few years ago, there was a lot of talk about being in the "river of God" and churches were experiencing flows of the Spirit like a mighty river that was sweeping them along. During that time the tangible presence of God was evident and, as a result, people's lives were changed. Many people, because of being in close proximity with His presence, started loosing control of their actions and experienced many different things. These actions were considered a sign of being spiritually blessed, which resulted in many of the effects being faked, or at least helped along with a little drama: if you didn't shake just right you were not getting the full blessing Then it all but stopped. Now you don't even hear anyone talk of the river any more. If the river of God is the Holy Spirit, did the Holy Spirit just dry up? I don't think so! I believe what happened was similar to almost every move of God we have had: people got so used to the signs of God's presence that we forgot about the One who was creating the signs. The very thing that was to draw us close Him became a barrier. People came seeking the signs of God's presence, but not God Himself.

I believe that God is stirring up His church, creating a hunger for Himself, that no signs can fill, only God Himself. When we come to the place where we really want only Him that is exactly what we will get. We have to get back to the "Garden," that place of total communion with God, as it was in Eden. The veil has been removed, our sins are forgiven, and now all that remains is to come to Him in Spirit and in Truth.

APPENDIX

When we look at Jesus on the cross we see a two fold sacrifice that was in the making right from the time of the fall in the garden. When God prevented man from eating from the tree of life in the garden, it was not because he did not want man to live forever, it was because if he ate of it in his present state he would never be able to come back into that eternal communion with God that he had before the fall.

In physics, Newton's third law states that for every action there is a equal and opposite reaction, and in the spiritual realm that is no different. Righteousness (a state of being in right standing with God) brings about life whereas sin (a state of not being in right standing with God) brings about death. The life that righteousness brings is eternal communion with God, whereas death is when our spirit and soul is removed from this body and we experience eternal separation from God. The cure for death, is a death as well. But not the death of a man who has an inherent sin from birth, no a man who is sinless. One who was in the sinless condition of Adam before the fall. Being that there were only two who where in that state before the fall, man and God, and man is disqualified by default due to the fact that he sinned in the first place, that left only one other. God Himself.

God knew right from the start that He was the only one who could bring about an end to death, and bring true life back to man. But in order for this to take place He would have to take on the form of man, become a second Adam, and pay the price.

God was looking for a people He could call His own, one with which he could enter into this world and do what needed to be done. And so came Abram, a man who listened to and trusted God, after all when God told him to pack up his belongings and head for a place he had never seen before, leaving everything he knew behind, he did exactly that. When God told him that his offspring would be as numerous as the stars, when he had no children and his wife was well past the age of giving birth, he believed God as well and it was accredited to Abram as righteousness. (Genesis 15:6)

God told Abram that his offspring would be His chosen people and He would be their God. He also told Abram that he would possess the land God brought him to.

God was not satisfied with just telling Abram about it He wanted to make it so solidified in his mind that it could never be shaken. So God spoke to Abram in a form that had been so significant to his culture from the time of Noah. God made a covenant with Abram.

In order to understand the significance of this you have to understand what a covenant meant. In the antiquities of the near eastern culture a covenant was one of the most important agreements that could be made. It was looked upon as being an unbreakable agreement, that had far reaching effects. Three aspects that were involved in making a covenant were first a sacrifice, then walking through the parts of that sacrifice, and the forming of a covenant scar of remembrance. There are other things that are involved in the process that will be discussed in another book, but for now we will concentrate on these three. The process of making a covenant was a process Abram understood very well.

> *"So the LORD said to him, "Bring me a heifer, a goat and a ram, each three years old, along with a dove and a young pigeon." Abram brought*

all these to him, cut them in two and arranged the halves opposite each other; the birds, however, he did not cut in half." (Genesis 15:9-10)

"As the sun was setting, Abram fell into a deep sleep, and a thick and dreadful darkness came over him" (Genesis 15:12)

"When the sun had set and darkness had fallen, a smoking firepot with a blazing torch appeared and passed between the pieces. On that day the LORD made a covenant with Abram." (Genesis 15:17-18)

When making a covenant a sacrifice would be cut into pieces and set in a pattern on the ground. The makers of this covenant would pass through the pieces and say "let it be done to me as it was to this animal if I should ever break this covenant." By giving the vision to Abram of the smoking firepot and torch going through the pieces of the sacrifice, God was solidifying His promise to Abram.

Another practice that was part of a covenant was the making of a covenant scar. This was normally done by slicing ones forearm and allowing a scar to form as a sign and remembrance of that covenant. Being that this covenant was about Abrams offspring, it was fitting that the covenant scar that God choose was that in the form of circumcision.

> *"This is my covenant with you and your descendants after you, the covenant you are to keep: Every male among you shall be circumcised. You are to undergo circumcision, and it will be the sign of the covenant between me and you."* (Genesis 17:10-11)

From this time forward God change his name from Abram to Abraham which means father of many.

Now lets jump forward in time to the cross and we see a fulfillment of this covenant in the form of Jesus Christ. Remember that God had chosen Abraham's seed to be the agent that He would take the form of man, enter the world as a second sinless Adam, to die and bring about an end to death's hold on our eternal separation from God. Here we find a virgin who was a descendent of Abraham's, who had never sexually been with a man, pregnant with a child that was conceived by being in the presence of God. This child grows up to be a man who chose not to disobey or remove himself from the influence of His Father (in other words he lead a sinless life by choice), which in turn fulfills what was required by the law in order to fix the problem that the first Adam created when he chose to disobey God.

When Jesus allowed Himself to be scourged, beaten, nailed to the cross to die, not only did He pay the price to eliminate deaths ability to eternally separate us from God, but He became the sacrifice for a New Covenant. This covenant, like the one between God and Abram, was made outside of man's involvement, and involves those who God has chosen as His people. His people of this new covenant include those of the first covenant, but also now people of all nationalities. Instead of a righteousness by works justifying us, righteousness that comes from faith in Christ brings us into right standing with God.

> *"For this reason Christ is the mediator of a new covenant, that those who are called may receive the promised eternal inheritance now that he has died as a ransom to set them free from the sins committed under the first covenant."* (Hebrews 9:15)

> *"For we maintain that a person is justified by faith apart from the works of the law. Or is God the God of Jews only? Is he not the God of Gentiles too? Yes, of Gentiles too, since there is only one God, who will justify the circumcised by faith*

and the uncircumcised through that same faith." (Romans 3:28-30)

"For there is no difference between Jew and Gentile the same Lord is Lord of all and richly blesses all who call on him, for, everyone who calls on the name of the Lord will be saved." (Romans 10:12-13)

There are many similarities and differences between the old and the new covenant, and there are many benefits that come from being under the new covenant. But these are to be discussed in another book.

Bibliography

Baker, Charlotte
On Eagles Wings
1990, Destiny Image Publishers, PO, Box 351
Shippensburg, PA 17257, page 46-47

Bonar, Horatious
RENT VEIL
1875, PDF Ebook, Mt. Zion Publications 2603
W. Wright St. Pensacola, FL 32505

Booth, William,
Why Should The Devil Have All The Best
Tunes?
http://www1.salvationarmy.org/heritage.nsf/0/
42d53ced9ec1583080256954004bff3e?OpenDo
cument

Brother Lawrence
THE PRACTICE OF THE PRESENCE OF GOD
1692, PDF Ebook, Feedbooks

Chambers, Oswald
MY UPMOST FOR HIS HIGHEST, UPDATED
VERSION
1992, Oswald chambers Publications
Associations Ltd.
Discovery House Publications, P.O. Box 3566
Grand Rapids, MI 49501, July 20, Jan 18

Dolphin, Lambert: Kollen, Michael
ON THE LOCATION OF THE FIRST AND
SECOND TEMPLES IN JERUSALEM http://
www.templemount.org/theories.html

Murray, Andrew
ABIDING IN CHRIST
1895, PDF Ebook, Philadelphia, PA. :H. Altemus,
Chapter One

Manning, Brennan
THE IMPORTANCE OF BEING FOOLISH
2005, HarperCollins Publishers, 10 East 53rd
Street, New York, NY,
(Paraphrased quote from page 125)

Spurgeon, Charles, H.
SERMON #2182 Metropolitan Tabernacle Pulpit
1 Volume 37 www.spurgeongems.org

Young, William P.
THE SHACK,
2008, Windblown Media, 4680 Calle Norte,
Newbury Park, CA, 91320, Page 67

CPSIA information can be obtained at www.ICGtesting.com
Printed in the USA
LVOW040841170312

273456LV00003B/1/P